MY BODY BOOK

Mick Manning
and Brita Granström

W

Contents

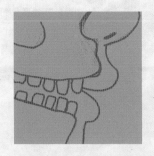

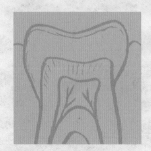

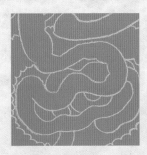

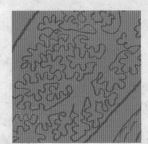

Welcome to your body!

Would you like to know how your own body works? Well, this book is all about *your* body, inside and out – so read on. Flip the flaps and sneak a look at what's happening under your skin!

BRAINS ARE BOSSY!

Let's start with your brain. It's inside your head and is always bossing your body around! It tells your lips to smile, your eyelids to blink, your nose to twitch . . .

In fact your brain has just made an order: 'Open this book!' That told the nerves to move some muscles, that moved bones, that moved your fingers to open the book and turn the page.

Now it's going to give your body another order: 'Flip the flap and look inside your head.'

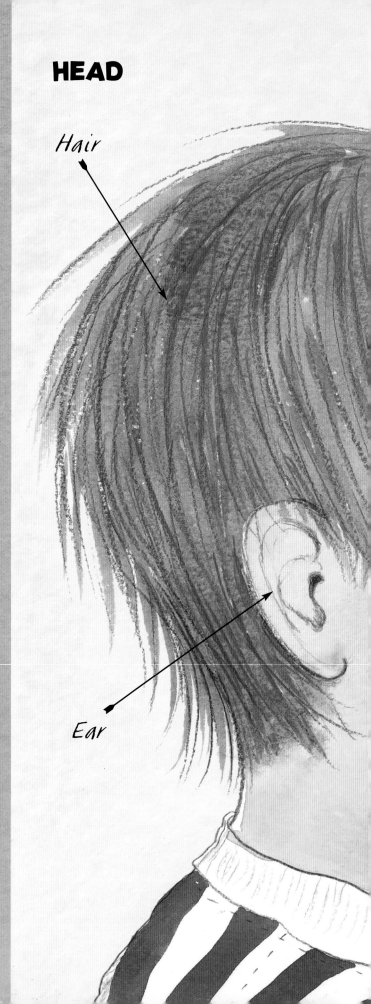

HEAD

Hair

Ear

4

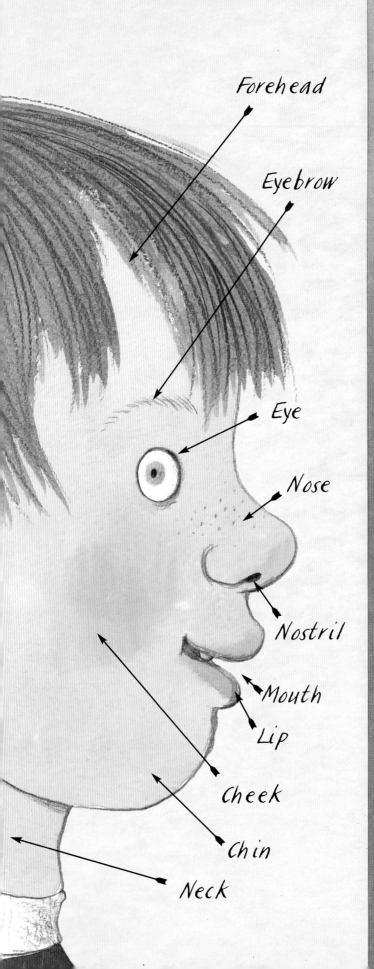

Forehead

Eyebrow

Eye

Nose

Nostril

Mouth

Lip

Cheek

Chin

Neck

NERVES

Nerves link different parts of your body to your brain. They look a bit like plant roots getting finer and finer as they spread out.

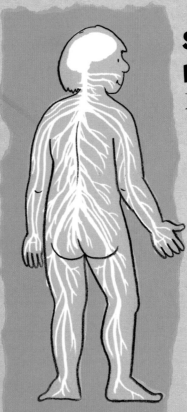

SENDING MESSAGES

Messages travel along these nerves to and from the spinal cord, a long nerve bundle that runs up your spine (backbone) to your brain.

LEARNING

Every time you learn something a new nerve 'path' is made inside your brain. The more you experience something, the better these new nerve paths get! It's like a weedy path that gets clearer and clearer every time your thoughts 'walk' there!

Smell it!
See it!

SIGHT

Eyes let you see the world you live in. They face forward, both looking at the same object at the same time but from slightly different positions. That helps you judge distances – useful when catching a ball.

Some people's eyes don't work properly – spectacles or glasses can help. They have plastic or glass lenses inside. Your eyes have lenses inside them too, flip the flap and see!

Smell goes in via the nostril

SMELL

You smell when you sniff air into the higher part of your nose. Here there are nerves covered with tiny hairs and 'snot'. The nerves 'sample' the air and send messages up to your brain which recognises smells – or learns new ones.

Want to look inside my eye?

EYES

Your eye muscle (the iris) adjusts the size of the black hole at its centre (the pupil). It makes the hole bigger or smaller so the right amount of light shines through the lens. The lens then focuses this light on the back of your eye, the retina. It's a bit like a cinema screen but the picture is upside down!

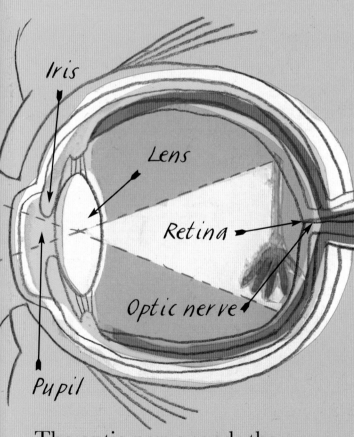

Iris

Lens

Retina

Optic nerve

Pupil

The optic nerve sends the upside-down picture to your brain, which turns the image the right way up!

What colour are your eyes? It's the iris that gives them their colour.

Brown

Green

Blue

7

Touch it!
Taste it!
Hear it!

TOUCH

When you touch something you 'feel it' with your sensitive finger tips. Nerves send messages to your brain explaining the sensation – it may be rough or smooth, lumpy or wet, hot or cold . . .

TASTE

Your tongue is a sloppy taste machine! It's covered with taste buds arranged to pick up different tastes – salty, sweet, bitter and sour. Try some taste sensations. Lick a salty crisp and then a sour lemon – blagh!

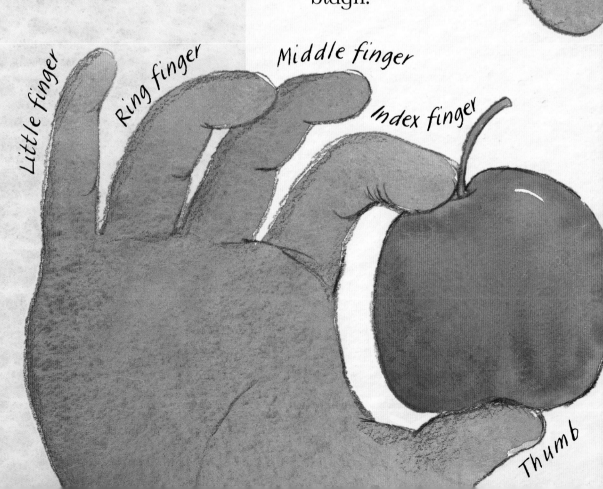

Little finger

Ring finger

Middle finger

Index finger

Thumb

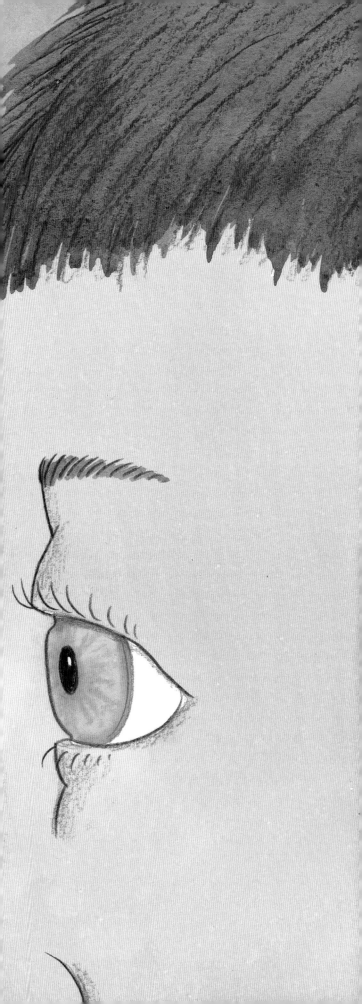

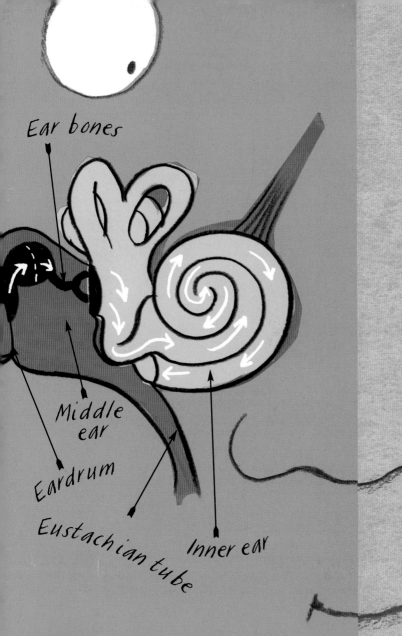

Ear bones

Middle ear

Eardrum

Eustachian tube

Inner ear

POP

Your ears go 'pop' sometimes when you're in a car or plane because of sudden changes in the air pressing on the Eustachian tube. The tube keeps the air pressure the same inside your ear as it is outside.

HARD OF HEARING

Some people's ears don't work properly – they can wear a small loudspeaker in their ear called a hearing aid.

DIZZY

The inner ear helps you balance. The liquid in it warns your brain about any movement. If you spin round quickly, all the movement signals confuse your brain. You get dizzy and fall over!

I taste my apple and hear it go crunch!

On the move!

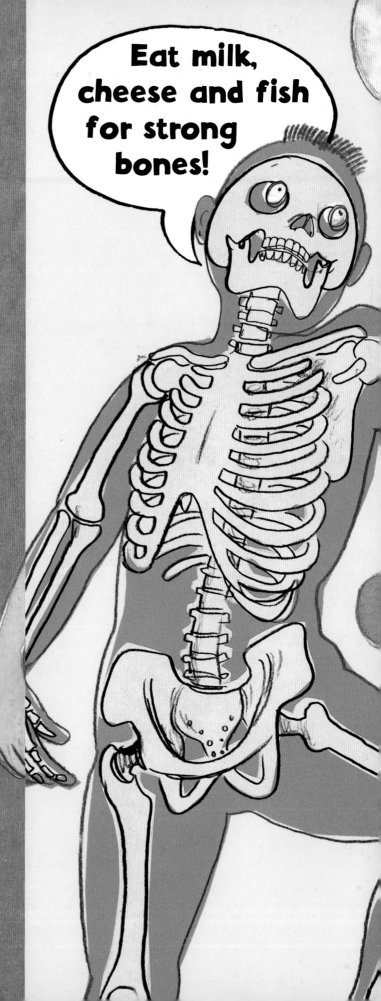

SKELETON

From long leg bones to tiny ear bones, bones are hard, strong and grow with you. You have 206 bones that join up to make your skeleton. This is your body's framework – without it you'd be like a wibbly, wobbly jellyfish! Joints join your bones together and allow you to move.

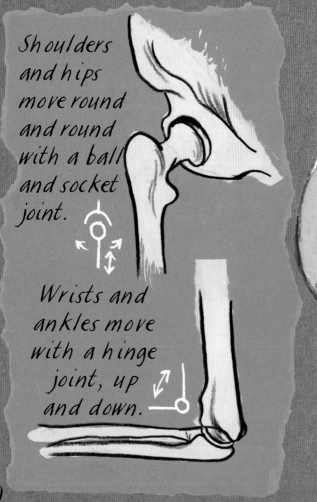

Shoulders and hips move round and round with a ball and socket joint.

Wrists and ankles move with a hinge joint, up and down.

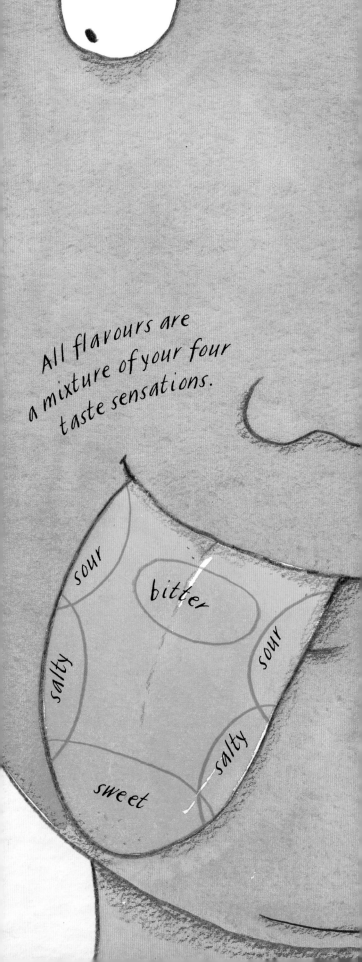

All flavours are a mixture of your four taste sensations.

sour

bitter

salty

sour

salty

sweet

HEARING

Your ear flap catches sound as it moves through the air and funnels it into your 'ear hole'. The sound hits your eardrum, a tightly stretched piece of skin, and makes it vibrate like a drum.

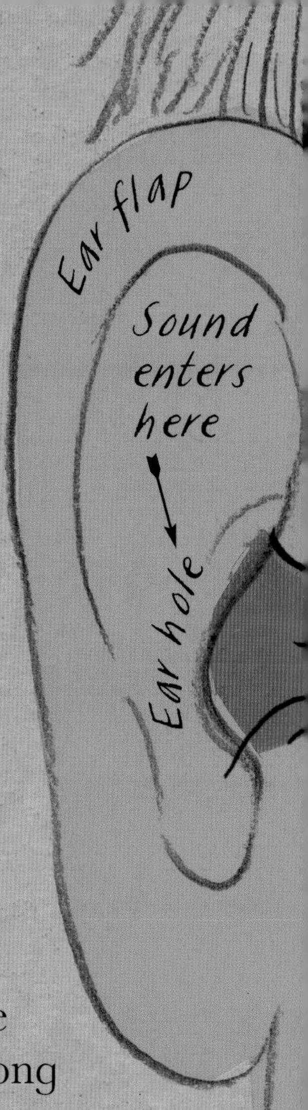

Tiny bones in the middle ear vibrate and this passes along to the inner ear, a sort of snail-shell shape filled with liquid.

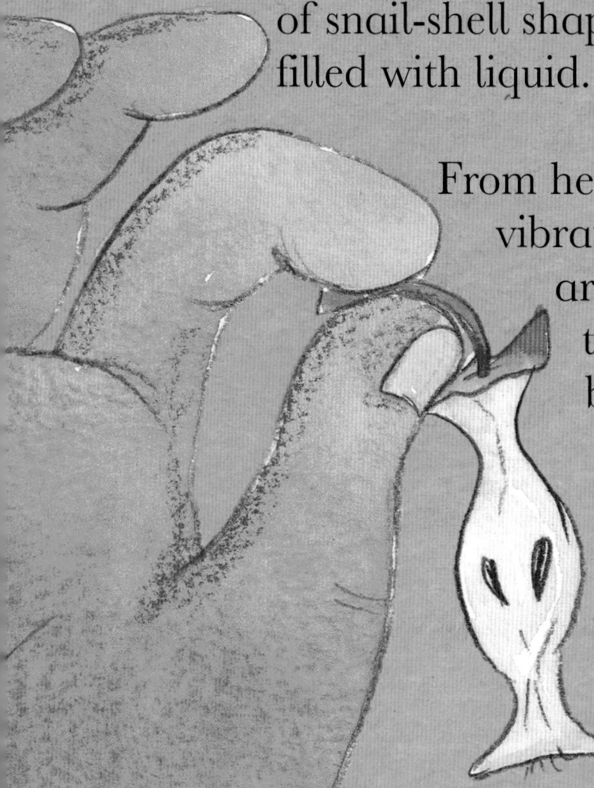

From here the vibrations are sent to the brain which decide what sound they are.

Ear flap

Sound enters here

Ear hole

...SCLES

...le please! You've just
...ed 17 muscles ...
...cles are arranged in
...rs under your skin. They
...attached to your bones by
...g 'elastic bands' called
...ns, which pull on the
...s when you tense your
...cles. Without muscles you
...dn't be able to move
...t, they help you walk,
...ven blink ...

Muscle tensed - bends your arm.

Muscle relaxed - straightens your arm.

Hair, voice and teeth

HAIR

Hair keeps you warm. It grows all over your body apart from the soles of your feet and palms of your hands. Hair is growing all the time – that's why you need haircuts. Some hairs fall out but new ones grow. Sometimes as adults grow older hairs stop growing leaving 'bald patches'.

Hair roots grow in tubes in your skin called follicles.

Sweat gland (see page 20)

Nerve

Follicle

VOICE

You can speak because of your vocal cords. These are flaps inside your throat. When you speak, air from your lungs makes the vocal cords vibrate which make sound. You can tighten or relax the vocal cords to make different sounds.

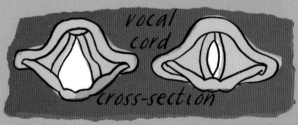

vocal cord

cross-section

These sounds go up your throat and come out of your mouth; but they need your teeth and tongue to turn them into words . . .

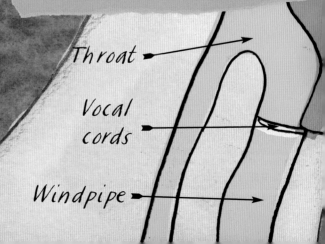

Throat

Vocal cords

Windpipe

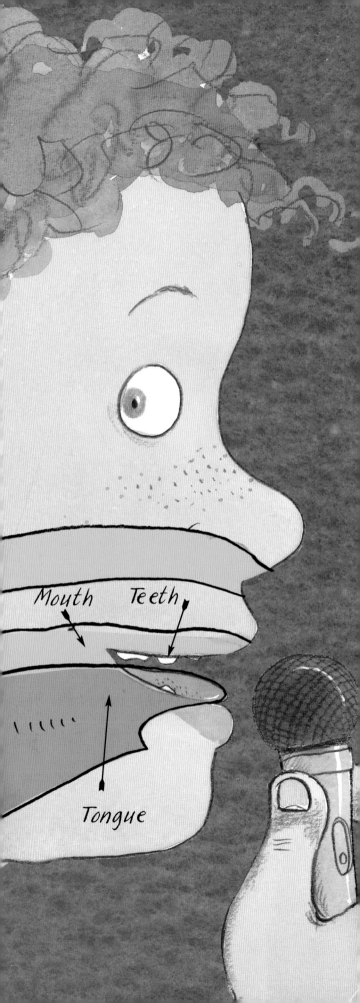

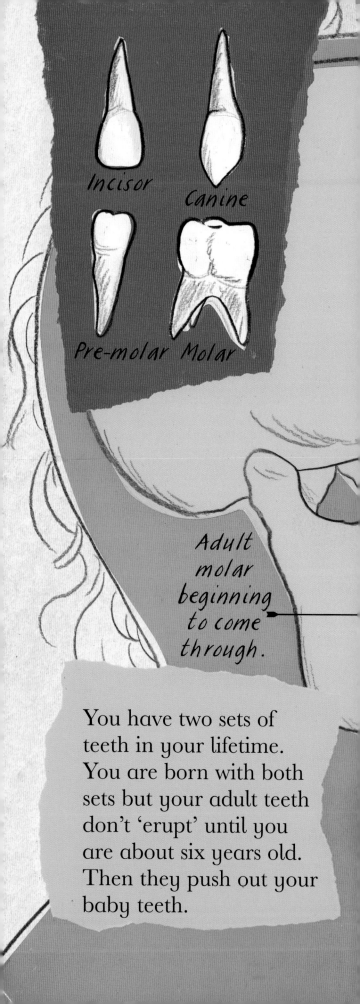

Incisor

Canine

Pre-molar

Molar

Adult
molar
beginning
to come
through.

You have two sets of
teeth in your lifetime.
You are born with both
sets but your adult teeth
don't 'erupt' until you
are about six years old.
Then they push out your
baby teeth.

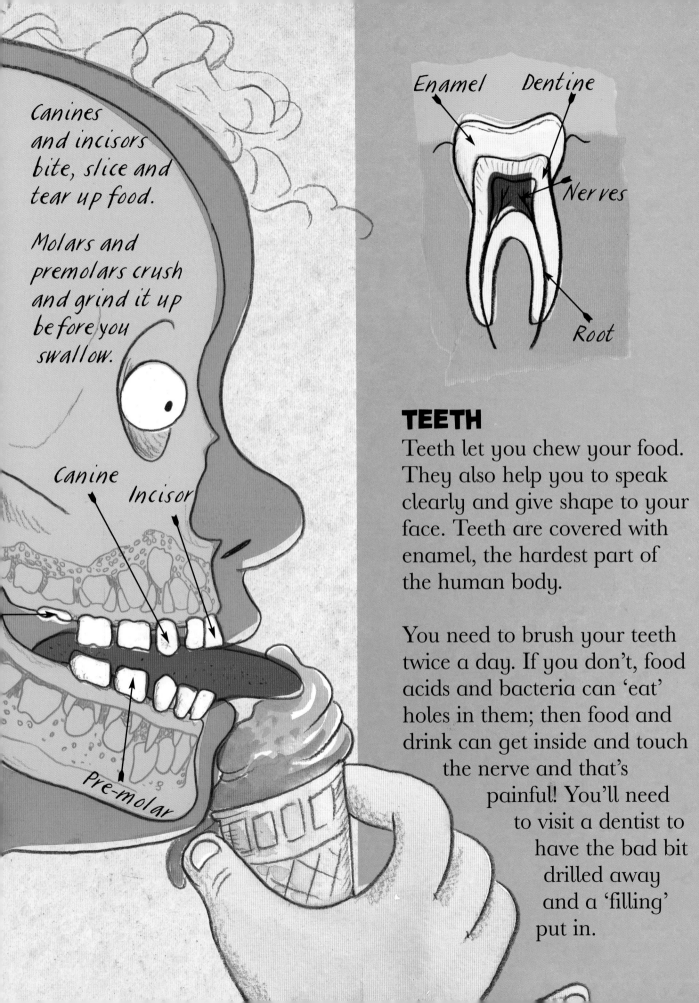

Canines
and incisors
bite, slice and
tear up food.

Molars and
premolars crush
and grind it up
before you
swallow.

Enamel   Dentine

Nerves

Root

Canine

Incisor

Pre-molar

TEETH

Teeth let you chew your food.
They also help you to speak
clearly and give shape to your
face. Teeth are covered with
enamel, the hardest part of
the human body.

You need to brush your teeth
twice a day. If you don't, food
acids and bacteria can 'eat'
holes in them; then food and
drink can get inside and touch
the nerve and that's
painful! You'll need
to visit a dentist to
have the bad bit
drilled away
and a 'filling'
put in.

Rumbly tummy

You must eat and drink to stay healthy. Food contains the fuel that your body needs to work but your body has to digest it (liquidise it) to take out the fuel. Every time you swallow food, you are sending it on a long journey through your digestive system, which starts in your mouth and ends in the toilet!

CHEWING

Your mouth is like a food blender! When you chew, your teeth and tongue break food up and mix it with saliva – that starts to dissolve it.

GULP

When you swallow the mush, it goes down your throat and into your food pipe. This muscly tube squeezes your food down to your stomach.

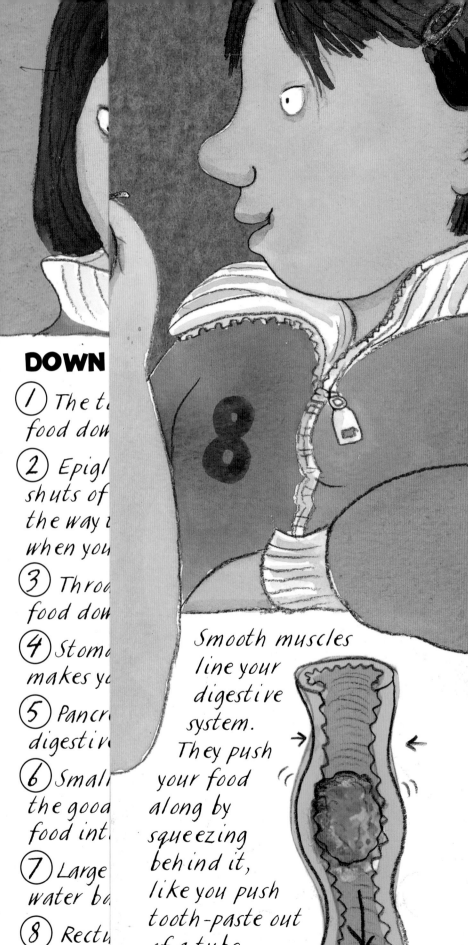

THE TUMMY

Your food goes down your food pipe to your tummy, or stomach. It's a stretchy sack which churns up your food with digestive juices to make a sort of lumpy 'soup'.

INTESTINES

The soup is then squeezed through your intestines – which are 7 metres long! They take out the goodness and water in food from the juices and into your blood, which carries them around your body.

OUT THE END

Your rectum is your body's own rubbish bin! All the lumpy waste from the food you have digested collects there where it is squeezed out as Waste liquid is stored bag called the bladder when it is full enough it squirted out as wee.

DOWN

1. The tube food dow

2. Epigl shuts of the way when you

3. Throa food dow

4. Stoma makes y

5. Pancr digestiv

6. Small the good food int

7. Large water ba

8. Rectu waste un

Smooth muscles line your digestive system. They push your food along by squeezing behind it, like you push tooth-paste out of a tube.

Feel your heartbeat!

Your blood is constantly moving around your body. It's pumped along by a muscle that never stops working – your heart. You hear and feel it as a 'heartbeat'. You probably notice it most when you are on the move but you can feel your pulse by gently pressing your fingers to the vein on your wrist anytime.

Your pulse is blood surging around your body each time your heart beats.

① Brigh[...]
the hea[...]
artery. [...]
the lun[...]
smaller [...]
branch [...]

② The [...]
goodness [...]
your boa[...]
intestin[...]

③ Oxyge[...]
of the b[...]
Waste pa[...]
includin[...]

④ The [...]
red (blu[...]
It pushes [...]
take it [...]

⑤ Next [...]
arteries [...]
the lung[...]
dioxide [...]
new oxyge[...]

⑥ Now t[...]
red agai[...]
around y[...]

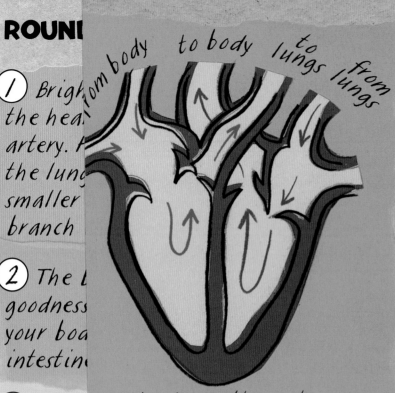

from body   to body   to lungs   from lungs

Blood goes through your heart twice on each journey round the body.

CIRCULATION

Blood's journey around your body is called 'the circulation' because it always comes back to your heart. Your blood moves along tiny tubes called vessels (arteries and veins). Imagine these are like a railway track and the blood is the train, dropping off and picking up passengers on its journey around the body.

[...]E BLOOD

[...]ssengers' your blood
[...]nclude the goodness
[...]r food (your body's
[...] the oxygen from the
[...]r body uses the oxygen
[...]p the fuel, which gives
[...]energy to live. This
[...]astes, including carbon
[...] more passengers for
[...] to carry away!

[...]made of liquid called
[...]. It picks up and
[...]uel and waste but it
[...]ies millions of tiny
[...]with other jobs to do.

Red cells carry oxygen to all parts of the body.

[...]s are

[...]cking
[...]de

Platelets stick together to make clots to stop a cut bleeding.

Take a deep breath

Breathe in and feel your ribs move out as your lungs fill up! Your lungs are two fleshy stretchy sacks filled with tiny air tubes. Every time you breathe your chest muscles move your ribs up and out to help your lungs fill with air. You need oxygen from the air to make your body work. Look back at page 17 to find out why.

INTO THE LUNGS

When you breathe air goes down your windpipe into the two 'air bags' we call your lungs.

Don't forget to breathe!

BRANCHING OUT

Inside the lungs, the air tubes branch out, getting smaller and smaller until they end in tiny air sacs, which are wrapped in blood vessels. The oxygen passes into the blood to be pumped round the body by your heart.

OUT AGAIN

While oxygen passes into the tiny blood vessels, waste carbon dioxide passes out of them back into the lungs to be breathed out in your next breath – clever eh?

You breathe automatically most of the time – swimmers have to learn to hold their breath under water.

You breathe about 16 times a minute, but you breathe faster when you are exercising. This is because your body needs more oxygen from the air to make more energy to work harder!

...und

...very air sac.

Skin tight

The final layer of your body is the one you see – your skin. Skin is amazing, a waterproof, stretchy covering that fits you like a glove.

Your skin contains blood vessels, nerves, glands and hair roots (see page 12). Skin also has tiny holes in it, called pores. When you get hot, the pores open to let out waste water called sweat. As the sweat dries off, it takes away some of your body's heat and cools you down.

Sweat keeps you cool but it can also make you smelly so you need to wash it off!

Slap on the suncream!

SKIN COLOUR

Skin contains melanin. This is a pigment that acts like a filter to protect skin from the sun's dangerous rays. People whose ancestors come from hot, sunny countries have more melanin in their skin – and the more they have the darker their skin. This is why people come in all sorts of colours!

However much melanin your skin has, it still needs protection from the hot sun. Make sure you put on sun block cream on sunny days.

MAKING DUST

Tiny little pieces of skin flake off your body all the time. They form a lot of the house dust we hoover up! But don't worry, skin always replaces itself. Even when you cut or graze yourself, new skin grows back.

Bodies are wonderful

So now you can say 'I've seen inside my body!'. But let's just remind that bossy brain of yours, one more time, about all the wonderful things everybody's body can do.

Eyes see words and the brain learns to make sense of them.

Noses smell everything – and the brain remembers the sweet and the stinky!

Ears hear sounds – and your brain enjoys them!

Bones help us stand, walk, run and play!

Muscles lift, pull, push and let us wiggle!

22

Hair is always growing.

Blood fights germs – even babies fight off disease.

Our digestive system turns food into 'body fuel.'

Lungs are always breathing.

Hearts tick like pocket watches – 70 beats a minute.

New skin grows and old skin becomes house dust!

Index

For Max, Björn and Frej with love, Mum and Dad

This edition published in 2008 by Franklin Watts, 338 Euston Road, London, NW1 3BH

Franklin Watts Australia
Level 17/207 Kent Road,
Sydney, NSW 2000

Text and illustrations © 2006
Mick Manning and Brita Granström

Brita made the illustrations for this book

Find out more about Mick and Brita on www.mickandbrita.com

Editor: Rachel Cooke
Art director: Jonathan Hair
Consultant: Peter Riley

Printed in China
A CIP catalogue record is available from the British Library.

Dewey Classification: 612

ISBN: 978 0 7496 8262 0

Franklin Watts is a division of Hachette Children's Books, an Hachette Livre UK company.